James Monroe

American Statesman

Colonial Leaders

Lord Baltimore
English Politician and Colonist

Benjamin Banneker
American Mathematician and Astronomer

Sir William Berkeley
Governor of Virginia

William Bradford
Governor of Plymouth Colony

Jonathan Edwards
Colonial Religious Leader

Benjamin Franklin
American Statesman, Scientist, and Writer

Anne Hutchinson
Religious Leader

Cotton Mather
Author, Clergyman, and Scholar

Increase Mather
Clergyman and Scholar

James Oglethorpe
Humanitarian and Soldier

William Penn
Founder of Democracy

Sir Walter Raleigh
English Explorer and Author

Caesar Rodney
American Patriot

John Smith
English Explorer and Colonist

Miles Standish
Plymouth Colony Leader

Peter Stuyvesant
Dutch Military Leader

George Whitefield
Clergyman and Scholar

Roger Williams
Founder of Rhode Island

John Winthrop
Politician and Statesman

John Peter Zenger
Free Press Advocate

Revolutionary War Leaders

John Adams
Second U.S. President

Ethan Allen
Revolutionary Hero

Benedict Arnold
Traitor to the Cause

King George III
English Monarch

Nathanael Greene
Military Leader

Nathan Hale
Revolutionary Hero

Alexander Hamilton
First U.S. Secretary of the Treasury

John Hancock
President of the Continental Congress

Patrick Henry
American Statesman and Speaker

John Jay
First Chief Justice of the Supreme Court

Thomas Jefferson
Author of the Declaration of Independence

John Paul Jones
Father of the U.S. Navy

Lafayette
French Freedom Fighter

James Madison
Father of the Constitution

Francis Marion
The Swamp Fox

James Monroe
American Statesman

Thomas Paine
Political Writer

Paul Revere
American Patriot

Betsy Ross
American Patriot

George Washington
First U.S. President

Famous Figures of the Civil War Era

Jefferson Davis
Confederate President

Frederick Douglass
Abolitionist and Author

Ulysses S. Grant
Military Leader and President

Stonewall Jackson
Confederate General

Robert E. Lee
Confederate General

Abraham Lincoln
Civil War President

William Sherman
Union General

Harriet Beecher Stowe
Author of Uncle Tom's Cabin

Sojourner Truth
Abolitionist, Suffragist, and Preacher

Harriet Tubman
Leader of the Underground Railroad

Revolutionary War Leaders

James Monroe

American Statesman

Brent Kelley

Arthur M. Schlesinger, jr.
Senior Consulting Editor

Chelsea House Publishers

Philadelphia

Produced by 21st Century Publishing and Communications, Inc. New York, NY. http://www.21cpc.com

CHELSEA HOUSE PUBLISHERS
Production Manager Pamela Loos
Art Director Sara Davis
Director of Photography Judy L. Hasday
Managing Editor James D. Gallagher
Senior Production Editor J. Christopher Higgins

Staff for *JAMES MONROE*
Project Editor/Publishing Coordinator Jim McAvoy
Project Editor Anne Hill
Associate Art Director Takeshi Takahashi
Series Design Keith Trego

The Chelsea House World Wide Web address is http://www.chelseahouse.com

First Printing
1 3 5 7 9 8 6 4 2

Library of Congress Cataloging-in-Publication Data

Kelley, Brent P.
  James Monroe / Brent Kelley.
      p.   cm. — (Revolutionary War leaders)
  Includes bibliographical references (p.   ) and index.
  ISBN 0-7910-5971-5 (hc) — 0-7910-6129-9 (pbk.)
  1. Monroe, James, 1758-1831—Juvenile literature. 2. Presidents—United States—Biography—Juvenile literature. [1. Monroe, James, 1758-1831. 2. Presidents.] I. Title. II. Series.

E372.K45 2000
973.5'4'092—dc21
[B]   00-038392
                                                                                      CIP

Publisher's Note: In Colonial and Revolutionary War America, there were no standard rules for spelling, punctuation, capitalization, or grammar. Some of the quotations that appear in the Colonial Leaders and Revolutionary War Leaders series come from original documents and letters written during this time in history. Original quotations reflect writing inconsistencies of the period.

Contents

James Monroe grew up on a farm in the colony of Virginia. Like the farm shown here, James's home contained many acres of fields and forests.

Country Boy

In 1754, Spence and Elizabeth Jones Monroe had their first child. The baby girl was named Elizabeth after her mother. Young Elizabeth was lonely once she learned to walk and talk. No other children lived for miles around her. But on April 28, 1758, a new member joined the family. A baby boy was born and given the name of James. Elizabeth now had a playmate, although it was a few years before she could actually play with him. Three more boys were born to the Monroes, but James was always Elizabeth's favorite brother.

The Monroes owned about 500 acres of farmland

and forest in Westmoreland County in the Virginia colony. Mr. Monroe was a farmer and a skilled carpenter. He built the large, two-story house the Monroes called home and made the furniture in it. The family was not wealthy, but their income was enough to pay the taxes and as a landowner Mr. Monroe could vote and serve on juries.

Toys and games were rare in the 1700s. Hide-and-seek was popular back in those times. Tag was another favorite game. There was also a game where one child hid an item such as a piece of clothing, a spoon, or even a rock. Then the other children had to find it.

Exploring was a favorite pastime. James and Elizabeth had a huge area in which to play. Often they spent an entire day just walking through the fields and woods. On days when the weather was bad, they stayed inside and played draughts (pronounced "drafts"). Both adults and children still play it today. We call it checkers.

James and Elizabeth were very close. They spent most of their time together. They played and shared the chores. It was important for everyone in the family to take care of the jobs they were asked to do. Some chores, such as chopping wood and plowing the fields, were too hard for the children. But they did many other jobs.

James and Elizabeth also studied at home. At first, their mother taught them. But as more children joined the family, there just wasn't enough time to teach the children. So the Monroes decided to hire a tutor.

James was a quiet boy, but he was very bright and a good student. He quickly learned how to read and write and do basic math. James and Elizabeth used math to keep track of the crop yields and the amount of lumber their father used in building houses.

The young boy also learned from his father.

L ike most other children, young James had chores to do. One kitchen chore was turning the spit that held meat over the fire in the fireplace. Turning the spit kept the meat from burning on one side and not getting cooked on the other.

Another chore was helping at harvest time. Corn, potatoes, and other vegetables had to be brought in from the fields.

Mr. Monroe taught James to shoot as soon as he was big enough to hold a **musket**. Hunting was one of the main sources of food in those days, and James became an excellent marksman.

In 1765, when he was seven years old, something happened that helped James decide what he was going to do in life. He overheard his father and his uncle, Judge Joseph Jones, criticize the British government.

The British Parliament in London, England, had just passed a new law, the Stamp Act. It said that the colonists had to buy special British stamps and attach them to all legal and business papers.

The law was really a tax. For the first time, the British Parliament had passed a law taxing the colonies. The lawmakers didn't even ask the people in the colonies what they thought about it. The colonists didn't think this was fair. People said it was "taxation without representation." George Washington was a member of the Virginia **legislature** at the time. He said that the Stamp Act went against the rights of Americans.

Hunting and fishing were important ways to bring home food during colonial times. James became a good shot at a very young age.

Patrick Henry was another member of the Virginia legislature. He and James's father wrote a **petition** against the act. The two men took their petition around Virginia and asked other people to sign it.

Many people in the colonies refused to buy the stamps. Eventually the British decided to **repeal** the Stamp Act. It was no longer a law.

Men in a tavern, reading and talking about politics. Politics was an important part of the conversation in James's home.

But the American colonists didn't trust the British government.

Politics became an important part of young James's life, and the topic was often discussed in the Monroe home. James read and reread all of the newspapers and pamphlets that his father brought home.

The leaders of the colonies stopped thinking of themselves as British subjects and began considering themselves Americans. George Washington, Patrick Henry, Spence Monroe, and other important men in the Virginia colony also referred to themselves as Virginians. These were thoughtful times and, years later, James would recall how the events of 1765 dramatically shaped his way of thinking.

At age 11, James finally attended a regular school. His father enrolled him in the Campbell-town Academy, which had only 25 students. The teacher was the Reverend Archibald Campbell, who taught Latin and math. James did very well in both subjects.

The school was a long way from his home and, for five years, he walked through woods and fields every day to get there and back home again. James would always carry his musket with him, to shoot birds, rabbits, and squirrels to take home for dinner.

While a student under Reverend Campbell,

James made his first friend outside his family. One of his classmates was a young man about his own age named John Marshall. The two boys were opposites in how they looked and acted. But they became lifelong friends.

When James was 14, something terrible happened. His mother died. His sister, Elizabeth, took care of the cooking and cleaning and kept an eye on her younger brothers. But losing their mother made the Monroe children very sad. They missed her.

Mr. Monroe was very unhappy about losing his wife. He loved her very much. Then just two years later, he died. James was 16 years old. He and his brothers and sister were orphans.

James left the Campbelltown Academy to take care of the things his father had done. His uncle, Judge Joseph Jones, was placed in charge of the Monroe estate.

Judge Jones saw that James was very smart and loved learning. The judge believed that the teenager had a great future in politics. Rather than allow his nephew to stay at home and become a farmer, he told James to keep going to school. He suggested that the young man attend the College of William and Mary in Williamsburg, Virginia. James could study law there.

James agreed. He sent a letter to the college describing his studies. The college accepted him as a student even though most of his learning hadn't taken place in a formal school.

The eager student began college in 1774. Up until then James had lived either on a farm or in a small school. At home he and his family had fireplaces for heating and cooking. They rode horses or small carts to get places. When it was dark, they used candles.

All of a sudden, he was in a large school in a city. The streets were filled with big carriages. He could pay drivers to take him places. Stores were everywhere, and James could buy cooked meals. People still used candles, but they also had glass lamps that burned oil.

Most of all, people were everywhere. At home,

it was possible to go days without seeing anyone but family members. Not in Williamsburg. The governor's mansion was in the city. The House of Burgesses met there as well. This was the group of Virginia colonists who made the laws.

Political issues were always on the **agenda** in Williamsburg. People could hear colonial leaders such as George Washington, Thomas Jefferson, and Patrick Henry talking about issues of the day.

These leaders often discussed what was happening in Boston—the biggest city in the colony of Massachusetts. Tea imported from England was being taxed and sold only to certain merchants. This made some men very rich and put other men out of business. People in Boston were very upset about this tax.

On December 16, 1773, a group of colonists dressed as American Indians had boarded British ships in Boston Harbor. They dumped nearly 350 chests of tea overboard. The "Boston Tea Party" was the way Massachusetts citizens let

To protest the tax on tea, colonists disguised as American Indians dumped chests of British tea into Boston Harbor. The event became known as the Boston Tea Party.

the British know that this tax had to stop.

When word of the Tea Party reached Britain, the British were angry. In 1774 the king closed Boston Harbor. Supplies usually traveled by ship, so with the harbor closed, people in New England couldn't get food and other things they needed.

The other colonies decided to help. They sent

food and money to Boston by road. The British didn't like that very much. To get back at the colonists, the British passed more harsh laws against all of America. They stopped travel between the colonies and placed taxes on everything being brought in by ship.

Members of Virginia's House of Burgesses discussed the idea of going to war against Britain. They sent word to the other colonies to send representatives for a first Continental Congress, which would meet in Philadelphia. Judge Jones, George Washington, and Patrick Henry were representatives from Virginia.

Some of the students at William and Mary knew that trouble, maybe even war, was sure to come. A group of them, including James and his roommate, John Mercer, began to practice shooting guns and studying military tactics. These students wanted to be ready for war if they were needed.

In the spring of 1775, war broke out in Boston, and James wanted to do more. It was hard to keep studying when so much was going on around him.

Soon students and citizens in Williamsburg decided to take action. James was the youngest member of a group that raided the British governor's mansion. They took all the gunpowder, firearms, and other weapons they could find.

Finally, at the beginning of 1776, James left college and signed up to be in the Third Virginia Regiment. That summer, he was sent to New York. Fierce battles were taking place. James didn't mind. He wanted to fight for freedom.

James joined the colonial army and quickly moved up the ranks. George Washington later described James as a "brave, active, and sensible officer."

2

Soldier

James Monroe was promoted to lieutenant in the summer of 1776. He had just turned 18 years old, but he had a big job. He was leading fighting men into battle. The Revolutionary War was in full force. Neither side was winning, but the British seemed to be getting the best of the Americans most of the time. James fought in some small battles. Then, in late August, he was in a big battle.

James was with George Washington's 7,500 men when British general William Howe and his 15,000 troops beat them at Brooklyn Heights, near New York City. Washington and his men were nearly captured.

That would have been a disaster. The British would have beaten the colonies.

But on the night of August 28, 1776, Washington and his men escaped across the East River to Harlem Heights. This was not the kind of battle James had dreamed of fighting in. The close escape made Washington decide to change the way he fought the war. He kept his men away from big groups of British troops. The Americans would fight a lot of little battles instead.

Then in September, many British soldiers attacked Harlem Heights. The American troops had nowhere to go. Washington and his men fought hard and drove Howe's troops away. They didn't really win the battle, but they didn't lose either. That was very important because the colonists' **morale** had been low.

In October, Washington moved his army north to White Plains, New York. Howe was marching his men through the area. The two armies met and fighting broke out.

The Americans lost the battle badly. Many

soldiers died. To avoid more losses, Washington moved west into New Jersey. James was given an award for being brave, but he wished the Americans had won.

In December, Washington moved his troops into Pennsylvania, just across the Delaware River from Trenton, New Jersey. Trenton was defended by 1,500 Hessian troops–German soldiers fighting for the British. On Christmas Eve Washington and 2,400 soldiers attacked by surprise. The Hessians lost a one-hour battle and a thousand of them were captured.

No American soldiers were killed and only a handful were wounded at the Battle of Trenton. Winning

In December 1776, James Monroe was with George Washington in Pennsylvania. Washington planned to attack the Hessian troops across the Delaware River in Trenton, New Jersey. He asked for a few volunteers to cross the river before he came over with his army. This small group was to guard the roads into Trenton so no one could get through to warn the Hessians. James volunteered.

The Hessians tried to use two cannons on Washington's troops. James and his party defeated them and captured both cannons. James suffered a serious shoulder wound. When he recovered, Washington promoted him to captain.

this battle made the soldiers feel much better. James was one of the men injured. Because of a shoulder wound he received, James was out of action for a long time. While he healed, he served as an aid to General William Alexander.

James wanted to go back to the war, but he had to wait. Almost a year passed before he could see action again. Finally, he rejoined Washington in Pennsylvania. The American army had grown to more than 10,000 soldiers. On September 9, the Americans began fighting General Howe and his troops at Brandywine Creek. The battle lasted for three days. Many men were killed or injured. The British finally won, driving Washington, James, and the rest of the men back to Philadelphia.

The representatives of the Continental Congress were meeting in Philadelphia at the time. They were afraid that Howe and his army would take over the city. They escaped to Lancaster, Pennsylvania, and set up a new meeting place.

Howe kept marching toward Philadelphia

In December 1776 George Washington and his troops were victorious at the Battle of Trenton. However, James was wounded during the battle and did not see action again for almost a year.

with 9,500 soldiers. The American army tried to stop them at Germantown. Washington came up with a clever idea. He divided his men into four units. They would attack the British from four directions in the early morning.

Luck and the weather were not with the Americans, though. A very dense fog covered the area that morning. One unit got hopelessly

British general William Howe, commander of the British troops that marched against the colonists in Philadelphia.

lost. Another unit couldn't send signals because the fog was too thick. Only one of the four groups was able to fight the British. It was too small, and the British army was too strong.

When the **casualties** from the Battle of

Germantown were counted, 537 British had been killed and four captured. Only 151 Americans were killed, but 522 were wounded and 400 more were captured. Even so, the battle was a great morale boost for the Americans. They felt that bad luck caused the defeat. Everyone believed that Washington's battle plan was good.

The Americans had to retreat again. This time they stayed in Valley Forge, Pennsylvania. The troops suffered great hardship that winter. It was very cold, and food and supplies were scarce. Many of the men wrapped their feet in rags because their boots had worn out.

James also stayed at Valley Forge. He didn't see major military action until late June 1778, when Washington's army met the troops of British general Henry Clinton at the Battle of Monmouth, New Jersey. The armies fought for two days. It seemed that the Americans would win if they fought long and hard enough. Suddenly General Charles Lee ordered the American army to pull back. Washington was very angry that Lee stopped fighting. But the battle was over. The British continued marching toward New York.

James received another promotion. At 20 years old, he was promoted to lieutenant colonel. James loved coming up with plans for battles. He liked to figure out different ways to beat the enemy. He also wanted to have his own troops to lead into battle. But the higher-ranking officers never gave him the chance. The only reason they gave was that he was too young.

Instead, James was sent back to Virginia to try to talk young men into joining the army. James failed. He tried, but there just weren't enough young men willing to fight. They thought Americans wouldn't win the war and didn't want to be on the losing side.

While he was in Virginia, James met Thomas Jefferson, the governor of Virginia at the time. James and the governor became close friends.

The young soldier began studying law under Jefferson, whom he respected a great deal. James

American troops spent a hard winter at Valley Forge, Pennsylvania, with little food and few supplies.

admired all the things Governor Jefferson had done. With Jefferson's encouragement, James decided to try his hand at politics.

James studied law under Thomas Jefferson. Jefferson once described James as "so honest that if you should turn his soul inside out there would not be a spot on it."

3

Life in
Politics

James learned a great deal about government and politics while he studied with Thomas Jefferson in Virginia. He also became friends with another government leader, James Madison. James got many of his political ideas from Jefferson and Madison.

James would follow these ideas when the war ended. In 1781, the British surrendered to General George Washington at Yorktown, Virginia. But the peace treaty that marked the end of fighting would not be signed for another two years. America was free. It was time to build a new nation.

James always had great ability. As a **protégé** of

Jefferson, he became well-known and popular. In 1782, he ran for public office. He was easily elected to the Virginia House of Delegates. This job began his political career. Soon he became a member of the Continental Congress.

At that time, Spain claimed that its ships had the right to travel on the Mississippi River. But America disagreed. Men representing the United States and Spain met to talk about this problem. They decided that Spain should be allowed to travel on the river.

James was completely against this idea. He and some other people got together and worked to make the Mississippi River out of bounds to foreign ships. Their work eventually paid off. Laws were passed and then Spanish ships had to stay off the American river.

James joined with his friend Madison in support-ing a stronger national government. But both James and Patrick Henry were against the **ratification** of the U.S. Constitution. They wanted a strong national government, but they felt the Constitution as it was gave too much power to the Senate.

When James was a member of the Continental Congress, he joined in the many discussions about how the new government should be run.

While in Congress, James met Elizabeth Kortright, the young daughter of a successful New York merchant. Elizabeth, who was called "Eliza" by her friends and family, was only 17 years old when they met. James was 27.

Eliza was a quiet girl. She was also beautiful. She could have married anyone she wanted.

She chose James. The happy couple was married on February 16, 1786.

Later that year, James left Congress and settled down in Albemarle County, Virginia. He wanted to be close to his **mentor**, Jefferson. James also wanted to learn even more about how politics worked.

Before the year was over, James became a father. The baby girl was named Eliza Kortright Monroe, after her mother.

James didn't get bored with politics. In 1790 he ran for the U.S. Senate. His friends Jefferson and Madison helped him during the election. James won easily.

As a senator, James worked with Madison to fight Alexander Hamilton's plans to have a strong federal government that controlled almost everything. James was very good at coming up with plans for political battles. He got the help of people in the other states who also disagreed with Hamilton and the **Federalists**.

These men became known as **Republicans**.

They worked long and hard to fight for what they believed was right. They wrote articles for newspapers explaining why their ideas were good.

Washington was elected the first president of the United States. He had to decide how the new country would deal with other nations. Many people thought President Washington favored the British. They were afraid he would get the French upset with the United States. After all, the French had helped America win independence in the Revolutionary War.

Washington sent John Jay to Britain to represent the United States. Jay liked the British more than the French. The Republicans were afraid that sending Jay to Britain would upset the French even more. They thought France might want to stop being friends with the United States.

James shared these concerns. Because of that, he was given a new job. Washington asked him to be the minister to France. This meant that James would live in France and represent the United States to the French government.

The streets of Paris, France. From 1794 to 1796 James served as U.S. minister to France. His wife, Eliza, was very popular with the French people.

Washington thought James would keep the French government from getting upset. He also thought James would make other Republicans less worried. So James took the job in 1794.

There was one problem. James tried to keep a good friendship between the United States and France by talking about how much Republicans liked the French. But Washington was not a Republican and he did not like what James was doing. After two years, he told James to return to the United States.

James was very upset. He felt as if he had been fired. He didn't like the way the president was dealing with other nations. James attacked Washington's policies. He wrote an article explaining why he didn't agree with them. He also defended his own actions in France.

James stayed active in politics for the next three years, working mostly behind the scenes. Finally, in 1799, his friends told him that he needed to hold public office. He agreed and ran for governor of Virginia. Again, James won. He held that office until 1802. As governor, he showed the political world that he was good at running things and could take action when it was needed.

The same year James ran for governor, he and Eliza had another baby—a boy. They named him James Spence after James and his father. But the infant was sick and never got better. He died early in 1800. Both James and his wife were very sad. Eliza mourned the loss of her baby for months. James worked harder than ever at politics.

In 1800, Jefferson was elected the third president of the United States. Both James and Madison helped him win the election. The new president named Madison his secretary of state.

In 1803, President Jefferson told his minister to France, Robert R. Livingston, to buy a port on the lower Mississippi River. France controlled the area known as Louisiana, just west of the river. Spain was trying to keep American ships from getting to the Mississippi River. Jefferson thought that if the United States owned a port near the mouth of the river, American ships would have a clear right to be there.

Jefferson sent James, along with Livingston, to meet with Napoleon, the leader of France. They asked to buy a small piece of land from France. Napoleon told them that the United

Thomas Jefferson became the third president of the United States.

States had to buy all of Louisiana or nothing. He would not sell off small pieces.

The two men didn't have the right to make

such a purchase, but they agreed to Napoleon's offer anyway.

Back in the United States, the president approved the purchase. When news of the Louisiana Purchase was made public, everyone approved. James was highly praised for his part in it.

As a reward, Jefferson appointed James minister to Great Britain. He held that job until 1807. James got along well with the British. The British politicians liked Eliza's slightly **aristocratic** manner. They thought well of royal people and of people who acted like royalty.

The Monroe family had a big year in 1803. Another child was born. They named their baby girl Maria Hester Monroe. She was beautiful like her mother. Important people were always visiting her home as she grew up. Because of this, she was comfortable around anyone.

The British government still kept American ships from going everywhere they wanted to go. It would not let many American products enter its country. In 1806, James **negotiated** a treaty

As a reward for his part in arranging the Louisiana Purchase, James was appointed minister to Great Britain. He lived in London for two years.

with the British that eased those rules a bit. William Pinkney helped him with the process.

James spent a lot of time on the treaty. He worked very hard and believed he had made the best deal possible. He knew that some parts of the treaty were a problem. For example, it did not end the **impressment** of American men. But James and Pinkney tried to convince the president that the terms were the best possible.

President Jefferson didn't like the treaty. He refused to send it to the Senate for ratification. Because of that, the treaty never became law.

James was hurt and angry that his friend wouldn't agree to the treaty. He did not blame the president entirely though. His other good friend, Secretary of State James Madison, also did not like the treaty. Madison gave advice to the president about how to work with other nations. So James also blamed Madison for rejecting the treaty.

President Jefferson, Secretary of State James Madison, and James Monroe had grown apart from one another and were no longer good friends. To protest their political actions, James ran for president in 1808. Madison was also running.

James knew his former friend was the best man for the job. He also knew that he had no chance of getting elected. But he wanted Madison and Jefferson to know exactly how he felt. In the end, Madison did win the election, but James also made his point.

James Monroe was 50 years old. He was not ready to leave politics. But there wasn't anything for him to do in Washington, D.C. So he returned to the Virginia Assembly in 1810 and 1811. Later in 1811, he became governor of Virginia for a second time.

Things were not going well for President Madison that year. His Republican Party looked like it might split up. Meanwhile, the Federalist Party was regaining its strength. Madison asked Jefferson for advice. After a long discussion, the two men decided that they needed to bring James Monroe back to Washington. President Madison asked James to become secretary of state. James accepted the job and the three men became good friends again.

James had a very practical approach to politics. Younger congressmen greatly admired him. He worked well with the people in Congress. It didn't matter which party they belonged to. He got most of the congressmen to pass the programs Madison wanted to make law.

Then the War of 1812 broke out. Great Britain and the United States were fighting again. James's old desire to lead his own group of men came back. He was still an officer in the army. He tried very hard to get to fight in the war.

The American secretary of war at the time was John Armstrong. He made sure James didn't fight in the war. He didn't like James at all. Armstrong believed that James hadn't given Robert Livingston enough credit for his part in negotiating the Louisiana Purchase. Livingston was Armstrong's brother-in-law.

Two years later the war with Great Britain was still going on. The British had invaded Washington, D.C.

Although several steamboats were built earlier by other people, in 1807 Robert Fulton came up with the first successful steamboat. Named the *Clermont*, it made regular passenger trips up and down the Hudson River in New York.

During the War of 1812, Fulton began construction on a steam warship to defend New York Harbor. He died in 1815 before completing the project, and Congress paid for the ship to be finished. The steam warship was completed in 1817, and President James Monroe became the first president ever to take a ride on a steam warship.

They burned much of the city, including the White House. Secretary of War Armstrong was blamed for the disaster. He hadn't made good plans for protecting the city. President Madison fired Armstrong and asked James to take the job. James accepted and in doing so held two very important **cabinet** posts: secretary of state and secretary of war.

James liked having to do two hard jobs at the same time. He made people in Washington feel safe. He also began to change the way the War Department ran. But something very important kept James from finishing that job.

Madison was finishing his second term as president. In 1816, the obvious Republican to run for the office of president was James Monroe. So he became the party's candidate. If he won the election, he would become the next president of the United States.

James was elected the fifth president and led the country into the Era of Good Feelings. Here, he is holding a big party for the opening of the new White House in Washington, D.C., which was rebuilt after the War of 1812.

4

The Era of Good Feelings

The presidential campaign of 1816 had two main candidates. Rufus King was the Federalist candidate and James was the choice of the Republican Party. The Federalist Party was losing popularity and Rufus King had very little support. James won in a landslide. He was the first former senator to be elected president.

The previous presidential **inaugurations** had been held indoors. They had been crowded and confused. There was not enough room for everyone who wanted to be present. The room was so crowded that there was hardly space to move.

So in 1817, James held the ceremony outdoors. Everyone was much more comfortable. People could see what was going on. Every inauguration since has been held outside, rain or shine.

Voters especially liked two things about James: the first was his no-nonsense attitude; the second was the way he stuck to old-fashioned values.

James was even old-fashioned in the way he dressed. He wore knee breeches and buckled shoes. Those clothes had gone out of style when Washington was president in the late 1700s.

James faced a big problem as president. The White House had been destroyed by the British army during the war. People had begun rebuilding it, but they hadn't finished yet. So James and his family had to live in a different house until the new mansion was ready. There wasn't enough room for big social events. The Monroes couldn't hold parties the way a president's family should.

Finally construction was finished. On New Year's Day, 1818, the Monroe family hosted a huge public reception; they were officially opening the new White House.

Though it still had many active members, the Federalist Party was growing weaker every day. It was strongest in New England. During the War of 1812, people in these states had talked of **secession**.

James wanted to bring the country together. Right after he became president, he toured New England traveling in a horse-drawn coach. Everyone welcomed him warmly. Even many of his critics seemed glad to see him. A Boston newspaper was struck by the good mood James created everywhere he traveled. It called his visit the beginning of an "Era of Good Feelings." The term was picked up by other papers. It stuck.

Because the Federalists had been so soundly defeated in the election, James believed that having two political parties was bad for the country. For a few years, only one party really existed—the Republican Party.

But this one-party system created a problem that James had not thought of. With two parties, each party could pressure its members to vote a particular way. With only one party, there was nothing to keep congressmen from voting against their president. How could he make his ideas the law?

At first, James used his friendships with congressmen to get laws passed. Soon, he saw that friendships were not enough. If he wanted to get things done, he would need a new idea.

Then the idea came. James would choose important men who were popular with Congress to serve on his cabinet. William H. Crawford was named secretary of the treasury. John Quincy Adams became secretary of state. John C. Calhoun was made secretary of war.

James changed Richard Rush's job too. Rush had started as attorney general, but he was much too businesslike. James named Rush as minister to Great Britain instead and asked the friendly William Wirt to be his new attorney general.

James placed the four most important men from Congress in what he saw as the four most important jobs in the federal government. The men worked well together and helped James

Henry Clay proposed the American System–his plan to make the country stronger.

get laws passed.

The main issue faced by James in his first term was the "American System." Henry Clay from the state of Kentucky was the Speaker of the House of

Representatives. He had a plan to strengthen the country's ability to provide for itself.

The first part of the American System called for building roads and canals that would make it easier to connect the East and the West. The second part of the plan was to raise the **tariffs** on foreign goods. Clay thought that such a tax would protect American companies from having to compete with foreign companies.

James did not think much of Clay's ideas. He worried about the plan to build roads and canals. He didn't believe Congress had the power to do this. Clay did not give up. He convinced Congress to act on his plan. Six years after he became president, James finally agreed to some of the first part of the plan.

The second part of Clay's plan passed more easily. Tariffs on English cotton goods were raised by Congress in 1816. In 1818 the tariff on iron went up. Then in 1824, Congress raised tariffs on all foreign goods again.

James's first term as president was a good time

for the nation. Many issues were resolved during the Era of Good Feelings which lasted for the first three years. In 1818, Congress set the number of stripes on the United States flag at 13 to honor the original 13 colonies. Later that year, James settled a boundary problem with Great Britain. When the United States bought the territory of Louisiana, it disagreed with Great Britain over where the northern border was. In 1818, everyone finally agreed on a border. Spain controlled Florida, but it also owed the United States $5 million. James agreed to take Florida as payment for that debt, and the United States grew larger. These events went smoothly and made James more popular.

But then the Missouri territory applied for statehood. This request created a problem.

During James's first term, three new states had already been admitted to the United States. Mississippi became the 20th state in 1817. It was a slave state. That meant it was legal for people to own slaves there. In 1818, Illinois joined the union as a free state. That meant people couldn't own slaves there. A year later, Alabama became state number 22. It was a slave state.

Whether a state was a slave state or free state was determined by geography. States north of the Ohio River and the Mason-Dixon line (which divides the states of Pennsylvania and Maryland) were free states. States south of those boundries were slave states.

The Missouri territory was part of the Louisiana Purchase. It had been settled mostly by Southerners who were slave owners. Missouri applied for statehood as a slave state.

The United States had 22 states. Half of them were slave states. The other half were free states. The free states did not want to allow a new slave state into the Union. That would give slave states greater power in Congress than the free states had. Neither the Mason-Dixon line nor the Ohio River helped to solve the problem. These boundaries did not go as far west as Missouri. Bitter debates went on for a year.

Then Maine also asked for statehood. Maine

Slave families being separated by white owners. Slavery was an important issue that James faced as president.

was a free state. This simplified matters a great deal. If the United States admitted Missouri as a slave state and Maine as a free state, the number of slave and free states would still be equal.

But what about the issue of slavery? Sooner or later, the rest of the Louisiana Purchase would be divided into states. Would those states be slave or free? Both sides debated the issue. The argument made people very angry.

James felt it was wrong for him to enter the debate. People in those days didn't want the president to tell Congress what to do. So James only talked about this subject when someone asked him a question. But the entire country knew that he opposed slavery.

When Congress agreed to make Maine and Missouri states, it made another decision. The Missouri **Compromise** said that slavery wouldn't be allowed in the Louisiana territory north of the lower border of Missouri (except in Missouri). James would rather have had no slavery at all. But he agreed to this compromise.

These debates made some people want two parties again. They didn't agree with James and most of the Republicans. Old Federalists and unhappy Republicans tried to start another party.

They couldn't get enough people to make it work, though.

James was very popular. He decided to run for a second term as president in 1820. And because there was still only one party, no one ran against James.

When the election was over, James had won easily. He received every electoral vote but one. That one vote was cast by William Plumer, a delegate from New Hampshire. He voted for John Quincy Adams.

The inauguration of 1821 was one of the grandest events the city of Washington had ever witnessed. For the first time, the United States Marine Corps Band was invited to play at the event. It has played at every presidential inauguration since.

A portrait of President James Monroe, whose Monroe Doctrine is still used in American foreign policy today.

The Monroe Doctrine

In the early 1800s, Spain was busy fighting France. It didn't have time to take care of its colonies in Central and South America. Most of these colonies broke away from Spain. They became new nations.

The people of the United States understood the problems facing these new nations. After all, they had just gone through the same thing only a few years before.

Early in James's first term as president, Henry Clay urged the United States to recognize these new nations. James didn't agree with this idea until his second term. That's when he finally agreed to ask Congress to recognize the new nations. James changed his mind because of what was happening in Europe.

After France was defeated, its government needed a new leader. The winning nations met and agreed to put a king back on the throne. They were **monarchies** themselves, run by kings and queens, and they didn't want their countries being split apart by people who wanted freedom. Russia, Prussia, and Austria were the three main monarchies in Europe. They all agreed that they had to get rid of all forms of **representative government** in Europe. Other kings and queens in Europe agreed with them. These nations were called the "Holy **Alliance**," but they did some terrible things.

The United States wasn't sure what the Holy Alliance might do. Some people were afraid that it might try to help Spain take over the new nations in Central and South America. These fears grew when they learned that the new

French king had stepped in and put down a rebellion against the king of Spain. And that is when a rumor began. It started in Europe and spread to the United States. The rumor was that France would help Spain regain its old colonies in Central and South America.

When this rumor reached the United States, people were very angry. They didn't want these new countries to lose their freedom.

The news also upset Britain. That nation traded many things with these new countries. If Spain took them over again, that trade would decrease. It might even end.

The British had always been against the Holy Alliance. But they had trouble finding other countries in Europe to help them. So they asked the United States to be their **ally**.

The British foreign minister had an idea. He talked to Richard Rush, the U.S. minister to Britain. Maybe their two countries could get together and give a stern warning. They would tell the world that they wouldn't allow European nations to get involved in what happened in North and South America.

Rush took the idea to James. The president thought it sounded like a good idea. He asked Jefferson and Madison what they thought. They liked it too. They told James that he should go ahead with it right away. Jefferson thought that with Britain as an ally, the United States would not need to be afraid of other countries.

Secretary of State John Quincy Adams hated the idea. He argued that it wouldn't matter whether the United States made a joint warning with Britain or not. He said that the British, in their own self-interest, would keep European nations from becoming involved in North and South America.

Adams also told James that a strong stand by the United States alone would do two things. It would warn the European countries. And it would also let the British know that they should forget any idea of moving into North or South America themselves.

John Quincy Adams, the secretary of state under James Monroe. Adams was also the son of John Adams, the second president.

James thought very hard before he made this difficult decision. At first, he had leaned toward joining with Britain, as Jefferson and Madison had advised. But then, he also had great respect for Adams.

Finally, he acted on Adams's advice. On December 2, 1823, James gave an important speech to Congress. He explained his new policy. It promised all the independent countries in the Western Hemisphere protection from European countries. James said that no new colonies could be created in North or South America. The colonies that already existed could not take any more land. In a short time, this policy became known as the Monroe **Doctrine**. It is a policy still followed by the United States.

European nations didn't try to take over their former colonies in South America. But this was not because of the threats from the United States. It was because they feared the mighty British navy. It wasn't until the late 1800s that the United States navy was strong enough to defend North and South America.

The Monroe Doctrine didn't get the United States more places to trade with either. Europe still did most of the trading with South America.

If anything, at the time, the Monroe Doctrine made things worse between the United States and the new nations in Central and South America. These smaller countries were afraid of the United States because it was stronger than they were. They didn't trust their neighbor to the north.

James worked on and solved another large problem before he finished his last term as president. Russia insisted that it had rights to the Oregon Territory. In 1824, as the election was nearing, James held difficult negotiations with Russia. Finally the United States and Russia made a deal and Russia agreed to give up its claim to Oregon.

But another question still remained. Who would become the next president? There was no obvious choice.

Both James and Madison had been the secretary of state right before becoming president. So Secretary of State John Quincy Adams thought he should be elected. But four other men wanted the job as well: John C. Calhoun, William H. Crawford, Henry Clay, and Andrew Jackson. They all ran for president too.

Andrew Jackson received the most electoral votes, but no one received more than half the votes. This meant that the House of Representatives had to decide the winner. Speaker of the House Clay told the people who had voted for him to vote for Adams instead. That gave Adams enough votes to become the sixth president.

That election marked the end of the one-party system that James had thought was best for the country. Jackson's followers accused President Adams

James decided to be extra careful about good manners while he was president. He wanted parties at the White House to be as proper about how things were done as anything he had seen in Europe.

People living in Washington thought such parties were snobbish. It didn't help that Mrs. Monroe rarely attended because she was ill. She only saw the people she had personally invited to an event. The Monroes' oldest daughter, Eliza, usually served as hostess in the early years of her father's first term.

of promising Clay a cabinet post in return for his support. When Clay was named secretary of state, the party split into two groups.

James Monroe had finished his job as president. He left Washington and moved to his home near Leesburg, Virginia. He called the estate Oak Hill. For the next four years he was a **regent** of the nearby University of Virginia. In 1829, he was in charge of the Virginia Constitutional Convention, his last political office.

On September 23, 1830, James's wife Eliza died. She had been married to James for 44 years. James was very, very sad. He finally left public life for good.

James owed a lot of money because he had used his own money when he traveled and worked for the government. (The same thing had happened to his good friend Jefferson.) He was practically bankrupt.

The former president was in danger of losing everything he owned. He wouldn't be able to live at Oak Hill anymore. James was 72 years old. He knew he was too old to become a lawyer again.

James had never asked the government to pay him back for what it cost him to live in France and England while he was representing the United States. Now that he needed the money so badly, he decided to ask to be repaid.

The members of Congress thought James was asking for too much money. Andrew Jackson, who was now the U.S. President, did not like James. These two reasons caused Congress to act slowly.

Soon James was almost out of money, and he lost his home. So he moved to New York to live with his daughter, Maria. Finally, after more than a year of waiting, James was awarded $30,000. This amount of money was only half of what he had asked for. Congress made its decision just in time too. James did not live much longer. He died on Independence Day, July 4, 1831. He was buried in New

Before his death at the age of 73, James lived with his daughter Maria in her home in New York.

York, but in 1856 his coffin was moved to Richmond, Virginia, his home state.

James Monroe is remembered today for establishing the Monroe Doctrine. He was a

James Monroe's grave was moved to this peaceful setting in Richmond, Virginia, in 1856.

dedicated statesman who worked for his country all his life. He was one of the most popular presidents the United States ever had. The nation grew considerably under his great leadership.

GLOSSARY

agenda–a list of things to be done

alliance–an arrangement by which countries agree to work together because of a shared need

ally–a nation that has agreed to help another nation

aristocratic–of the upper class

cabinet–a committee of advisors or ministers serving a government

casualties–soldiers lost from military service due to death or injury

compromise–an agreement that settles a fight by having both sides give in on some points

doctrine–a belief or principle

Federalist–someone who believes in a strong national government

impressment–the act of taking men by force to serve on navy ships

inauguration–a ceremony during which a person is officially put in office

legislature–a group of people given the power to make laws

mentor–a trusted teacher or guide

monarchy–a country ruled by a king or queen

morale–the confidence a person or group feels about what they are doing

musket–a large gun used before the invention of the rifle

negotiate–to settle a disagreement by talking together

petition–a signed, written request asking for an action to
be taken

protégé–a person being taught and promoted by another person

ratification–the process of approving something or making it
official

regent–a person who serves on a governing board

repeal–to take back or make inactive

representative government–government in which the public
is represented by people chosen from among them

Republican–someone who believes in a strong state
government

secession–the act of withdrawing or breaking away from a
nation

tariff–a tax on imports or exports

CHRONOLOGY

1758   Born to Spence and Elizabeth Jones Monroe on April 28 in Westmoreland County, Virginia.

1765   Monroe family joins protests against the Stamp Act.

1774   Enters College of William and Mary.

1776   Enlists in Third Virginia Regiment; promoted to lieutenant; receives serious shoulder wound during the Battle of Trenton.

1778   Promoted to lieutenant colonel; sent to Virginia to recruit; meets Thomas Jefferson and James Madison.

1782   Elected to Congress.

1786   Marries Elizabeth Kortright; daughter Eliza Kortright Monroe is born.

1790   Elected to the Senate; the Republican Party is formed.

1794   Appointed minister to France by President Washington.

1796   Ordered back to United States from France.

1799   Elected governor of Virginia; son James Spence Monroe is born.

1800   Son dies.

1803   Helps to negotiate Louisiana Purchase; appointed minister to Britain; daughter Maria Hester Monroe is born.

1806   Negotiates treaty with Britain but it is turned down by Jefferson.

1808	Runs for president against Madison and loses.
1810	Elected to Virginia Assembly.
1811	Elected governor of Virginia for the second time; appointed secretary of state by President Madison.
1812	The War of 1812 begins.
1814	The British burn Washington, D.C., and the White House.
1815	Appointed secretary of war; the War of 1812 ends.
1816	Elected president; Era of Good Feelings begins.
1820	The Missouri Compromise is announced; elected to second term as president.
1823	The Monroe Doctrine is delivered to Congress.
1825–29	Becomes a regent of the University of Virginia.
1829	Becomes presiding officer of the Virginia Constitutional Convention.
1830	Wife Eliza dies.
1831	Dies on July 4 in New York City.
1856	Is reburied in Richmond, Virginia.

REVOLUTIONARY WAR TIME LINE

1765 The Stamp Act is passed by the British. Violent protests against it break out in the colonies.

1766 Britain ends the Stamp Act.

1767 Britain passes a law that taxes glass, painter's lead, paper, and tea in the colonies.

1770 Five colonists are killed by British soldiers in the Boston Massacre.

1773 People are angry about the taxes on tea. They throw boxes of tea from ships in Boston Harbor into the water. It ruins the tea. The event is called the Boston Tea Party.

1774 The British pass laws to punish Boston for the Boston Tea Party. They close Boston Harbor. Leaders in the colonies meet to plan a response to these actions.

1775 The Battles of Lexington and Concord begin the American Revolution.

1776 The Declaration of Independence is signed. France and Spain give money to help the Americans fight Britain. Nathan Hale is captured by the British. He is charged with being a spy and is executed.

1777 Leaders choose a flag for America. The American troops win some important battles over the British. General Washington and his troops spend a very cold, hungry winter in Valley Forge.

1778 France sends ships to help the Americans win the war. The British are forced to leave Philadelphia.

1779 French ships head back to France. The French support the Americans in other ways.

1780 Americans discover that Benedict Arnold is a traitor. He escapes to the British. Major battles take place in North and South Carolina.

1781 The British surrender at Yorktown.

1783 A peace treaty is signed in France. British troops leave New York.

1787 The U.S. Constitution is written. Delaware becomes the first state in the Union.

1789 George Washington becomes the first president. John Adams is vice president.

FURTHER READING

Bains, Rae. *James Monroe: Young Patriot.* Mahwah, N.J.: Troll, 1997.

Blumberg, Rhoda. *What's the Deal?: Jefferson, Napoleon, and the Louisiana Purchase.* Washington, D.C.: National Geographic, 1998.

FitzGerald, Christine Maloney. *James Monroe: Fifth President of the United States.* Danbury, Conn.: Children's Press, 1987.

Isaacs, Sally Senzell. *America in the Time of George Washington.* Portsmouth, N.H.: Heinemann, 1998.

Old, Wendie C. *James Monroe.* Berkeley Heights, N.J.: Enslow, 1998.

INDEX

PICTURE CREDITS

page

ABOUT THE AUTHOR

BRENT KELLEY is a veterinarian and writer. He is the author of many books on baseball history. Two books (written under the pen name Grant Kendall) tell about his experiences as a veterinarian. He has also written two books for Chelsea House. He is a columnist for *Thoroughbred Times,* a weekly horse racing and breeding publication. He also writes for *Bourbon Times,* a weekly family newspaper. Brent Kelley has written nearly 400 articles for magazines and newspapers. He lives in Paris, Kentucky, with his wife and children.

Senior Consulting Editor **ARTHUR M. SCHLESINGER, JR.** is the leading American historian of our time. He won the Pulitzer Prize for his book *The Age of Jackson* (1945), and again for *A Thousand Days* (1965). This chronicle of the Kennedy Administration also won a National Book Award. He has written many other books, including a multi-volume series, *The Age of Roosevelt.* Professor Schlesinger is the Albert Schweitzer Professor of the Humanities at the City University of New York, and has been involved in several other Chelsea House projects, including the COLONIAL LEADERS series of biographies on the most prominent figures of early American history.